FROM RAGS TO RICHES

by Dezarita Dashai

Illustration: by LeRoy Grayson
Publishing: by Jazzy Kitty Publication

Rags to Riches
By Dezarita Dashai

Cover Illustrated by Leroy Grayson
Published by Jazzy Kitty Publications
Logo Designs by Andre M. Saunders/Jess Zimmerman
Editor: Anelda L. Attaway

© 2021 Dezarita Dashai
ISBN 978-1-954425-12-5
Library of Congress Control Number: 2021902463

All rights reserved. This book is protected by the copyright laws of the United States of America. This book may not be copied or reprinted for commercial gain or profit. The use of short quotations or occasional page copying for personal or group study is permitted and encouraged. Permission will be granted upon request. This book is for Worldwide Distribution and printed in the United States of America, published by Jazzy Kitty Publications utilizing Microsoft Publishing Software.

DEDICATION

I dedicate this book to every person wanting more in life! God promised your life to be more abundant! So, begin to transition your mind to receive all your heart desires!

TAKE YOUR MINDSET FROM RAGS TO RICHES!
YOU DESERVE IT!

TABLE OF CONTENTS

INTRODUCTION	i
CHAPTER 1 – Since You	01
CHAPTER 2 – Hey Ma	08
CHAPTER 3 – I Imagine Myself	12
CHAPTER 4 – TRE	18
CHAPTER 5 – Let's Go Back	28
CHAPTER 6 – Fork in My Path	35
CHAPTER 7 – I'm Blessed	42
CHAPTER 8 – God Got Me!	49
CHAPTER 9 – Other Men	55
CHAPTER 10 – My First Apartment	63
CHAPTER 11 – My Dream Man	67
CHAPTER 12 – Louis	71
CHAPTER 13 – A New Place	76
CHAPTER 14 – How You Came About	81
CHAPTER 15 – Live Life to the Fullest	87
OUTRO	90

INTRODUCTION

Do you ever get tired of the life your living?

Do you figure it must be more to life than this?

Have you ever wondered if more people like you existed?

People who want to enjoy life and who could care less about what this world thinks.

WE want to LOVE because it feels good, no alternative motives! We just want to live life to its fullest! Always Reaping all that we deserve and desire and constantly eating the fruits of our labor.

Well, I Dezarita Dashai is that person who knows that God, Himself promised my son and me a better life. Therefore, why should I settle for less?

LIFE! A gift from God! It can't possibly be this and only this! I am 24 years old, and my son is four. As of today, we are leaving everything in the wind as we begin our journey to our FRESH START!

CHAPTER 1
Since You

I was born into abuse. As a toddler, my little sister was taken away by a 6 ft. 258-pound monster. He forced us into a system that doesn't love girls that look like me! The night we had to stay in that place that smelled like a hospital was horrible. A 5-year-old scared little girl blinded by bright lights, doctor hands, and instruments all over her body was so horrifying. The worst part was me crying out, longing to be assured that I was safe, loved and that everything was going to be okay. Instead, they laughed at me and insisted that I was overdramatic. They got irritated and left me there alone to soak in my misery.

As I remember how I use to settle for that life, it hits me. It's all about going from "Rags to Riches!" What -does that mean to you? I don't know, but it's a state of mind for me!

You see, six long years ago, I knew that life was destined for my son and me and was more than constant punches back and forth over bad attitudes. More than disrespectful words and actions. More than abuse aimed at the pits of our empty souls. The life that was promised to us played in my head like my favorite song, so sweet and settling to my spirit. It was out there fluttering in the darkest skies like a lightning bug longing to be captured.

Alone in my dusty old basement, the smell of mothballs filled the air as my belly echoed off the walls for food. Turning up my Gospel music to drown out the annoying yells, I continued to fast and pray, which gave me more willpower. As the rain fell from my face, I heard a faint voice say, *"Leave WISCONSIN!"* That was the voice of the Lord. Feeling confused yet, satisfied I pulled up a map, and TEXAS was smiling at me. Just like - that, I had made up my mind. We were moving to Texas, leaving Sunnyvale, Wisconsin!

When I was about seven years old, I was brought here by my Daddy with my older sister. My sister Shantel was nine, and she was so tough. They used to call her the bad one and me the good one. The truth is, she was never bad. She was the one who boldly expressed how life had already thrown her to the wolves. I was timid and scared of what had already happened.

Our Dad used to say, "The judge only gave me y'all because I was married to Taylor."

Taylor was Stepmother, who was an angel. We were demanded to call her by her name, but we never could. She raised us from little girls, and she was the only mom we knew.

Our first year being in Sunnyvale was cool. I remember because I was in second grade and had this fantastic Teacher! Ms. Quien at Tank Elementary. Every week, we'd have to write a story of whatever we pleased. I remember being so eager to get that pencil in my hand and drift off into my own little world. Picture a thin, short timid Black little girl with beaded braids down her back. It was a shy little thing that had so much to say on paper and so much love to give, even then. But very little to say to people. As we wrote, Ms. Quien was pleased to see the pain that I let loose onto paper. She'd always look at me with relief after I wrote. As if she could see the pain that I needed to let go of, that even my top layer had no idea it existed. She loved me, just because! That made me happy.

Coming from Chicago, Illinois, was a change that I don't fully remember. Flashes of my past come back to haunt me like a reoccurring nightmare. Sometimes I'd find myself sitting down, forcing myself to focus. I would sit for a long time trying to put a 1000-piece jigsaw puzzle together. It seemed as if the colors were always blending in together. In the end, my mind always started vibrating like a steel nail being hammered repeatedly. So, I didn't bother anymore.

We had a home-cooked meal every day. Our house was always clean, and we stayed looking good, all six of us. We were really happy. My favorite thing was that there was always a birthday party because there were so many of us. We had ice cream and cake with whatever else they decided to make. Then came the party and we danced, danced, and danced. Christmas was always fabulous because my Mommy made sure we got toys from the Salvation Army. Toys would be stacked up, almost covering the tree because it was so many of us. My Daddy would put this song on before we opened the gifts. We all would dance around; I held onto days like that because it felt so good just to be loved.

As the years went by, I reached middle school. I was 12 years old, and somehow, things changed. I'm not sure how, nor why. They just did when I ran out of people who loved me for no reason at all. Suddenly, it seemed as if the world got heavy. The abuse was back in my face as if it were a part of me. I caught my Daddy in a car in front of our house (a husband of 6 beautiful kids right upstairs) with another woman doing things a husband should only do with his wife. I was coming to ask him a question, and boom, there they were. He was with a friend of the family. She was supposed to be giving him a ride back to the house. Well, I guess she was in her own special way! After I caught him, there was no explanation, no talk, no nothing. I tried to quickly go back upstairs until I heard a simple demand.

"Go get me a beer."

I swallowed the knot in my throat and did as I was told. I was old enough to know that was not the way things were supposed to go, but not old enough to go to my Mommy and blurt out all that I had just seen. All I could do was continue to write. Then here come my siblings reading my - diary. They took it to my Mommy (Taylor).

I remember her saying, "OEEEEE," I am going to tell your Daddy."

Fear took over as I grabbed my journal, ripping it with tears flowing down my face! For years, this was normal for me every other day. My Dad was cheating on our Mother, having babies on her, abusing her as if she were nothing. I witnessed it all. But, after the one time, I did let some awful information loose. My Dad called me into the room, looked me right in my eyes.

He calmly said, "Stay in a kids' place, and if you don't, I'll ship your ass off."

The same day, we went out, and it was sunny. Me and my siblings were taken to Game World, a huge indoor gaming place. We were all so happy, caught up in the loud sounds from the machines and hundreds of laughs from children. Then a strong hand tapped me on the shoulder.

Asking me a question I never thought I hear, "How it feels to be a kid?"

I replied, "Good."

The voice said with such sternness, "Good! Keep it that way."

For a moment, I was confused, thinking, *"I don't go looking for the mess. I will just be minding my own kid life. Then, I see you doing what you do. I tried my best to be a kid."*

And from that moment, all I could do was write and hide my diary to maintain my wholeness. There was a feeling I felt; it felt like the life I had was being ruined. I wanted so badly to tell him to kick rocks, but instead, all I did was write.

"SINCE YOU"

SINCE YOU

Raised me,

You figured you can Shrink me

SINCE YOU

Beat me,

You figured I'd Fear you

SINCE YOU

Brought me into this World,

You figured you can Take Me Out

SINCE YOU

DON'T Respect me,

You figured I BETTER Respect you

SINCE YOU

Hate our family,

You figured I should Hate them Too

SINCE YOU

Are NOT Happy,

You figured I WON'T BE

BUT BOY, LET ME TELL YOU THIS…

SINCE I GOT A LIFE, I FIGURE

YOU NEED TO GET ONE INSTEAD OF RUINING MINE!

CHAPTER 2

Hey Ma

I used to dream of my Mama (My Birth Mother) when I had no one to talk to but God and a piece of paper. Often, she is in the back of my mind, imagining that I would run to her as she scooped me up. Then she would repeatedly be apologizing for all the pain she caused me. I would forgive her, and we would be the best of friends. She would rescue me from my heartbreaking each day as I saw my Dad hurt his wife, my Mother! The one who took me in as her own! That was my go-to dream amid tears drowning my aching pain. But that's all it was, just a dream. After we were taken away from her, we may have seen Mama about two more times before she was untraceable.

My freshman year in high school, Mommy had finally realized her worth. Mommy was such a strong woman, both physically and mentally. She could do everything and was a strong warrior in her faith. My Mom had to be because I never seen her once shed a tear. She was always so happy. I mean, we had family night faithfully. Other folks even dropped their kids off to get in on the action. She was there for every one of my milestones, being very proud of me. Mommy kept us in church, read the Bible to us daily, and poured that good ol' Gospel music into us. She installed into us so many beautiful morals. I carry all of them to this day! I sincerely thanked the judge so much for awarding us to her. Well, that was until she divorced my Dad and moved back to Chicago with her family. My sister Shantel and I were not legally hers, so we were stuck and could not go with her. She only took my two brothers and two sisters when she left. Therefore, our beautiful family bond was broken that day! After that,

I felt motherless and fatherless; I ended up jumping from house to house. Sometimes with family, friends, or wherever I could lay my head. Everyone had their own life, my family included. I was too much baggage for them because they had their own problems. So, I always understood why I didn't stay in one spot for too long.

My sister Shantel became pregnant at 16; she brought a beautiful baby boy into this world. Although we weren't close, she gave me the honor of naming him.

When Shantel was about to give birth, it was like a huge party in her delivery room. I mean, my aunties, cousins, and my Dad brought in bottles of alcohol. I'm not sure how my sister felt about that, but the room was lit. When it came time for her baby boy to come out, I was so happy because I cut the cord. Everyone was so proud of her and passed the baby around, giving him love.

But then reality set in, and she was back in the life we were thrown into. Soon after, they took her baby and put him in the system. I know that hurt my sister and gave her more reason to be angry at the world. She was in and out in juvenile detention because she was so angry, and she had a right to be! Her anger showed every time you looked at her. I on the other hand, was severely depressed and broken, except no one could tell. I learned how to say to people what they wanted to hear and mask my pain as if none existed. I was convinced that no one wanted the truth because it was way too ugly. Hell, I even tried running from it.

This thing called "staying in a kids' place" is so much easier said than done! I was forced out of that title a long time ago. You see that daddy of ours couldn't take care of us, never could. As he said, the judge only gave us to him because he was married. I began to think, *"What if our Birth Mama hadn't allowed such abuse from her boyfriend; what if she didn't allow him to hit us or lock us in rooms as we grew hungry? What if she didn't allow us to gain scars all over our body, for which we never got an explanation. I wonder if that Monster hadn't killed our sister, would my shoulders feel so heavy at the age of 14?"*

The most my Daddy did was register me for school and left the rest up to whomever. What else could he do? Half the time, I didn't know where he stayed and what woman was with him. I just knew he was in the same small town as me. I just knew that I needed him to explain this all to me, to ask me how I felt, and to tell me it all was going to be okay. However, that wasn't an option.

I was barely making it academically in class because my world that I had known had fallen apart. The family of four girls and two brothers that made my world okay at the end of each awful day was broken. I didn't want to be at school; I wasn't interested at all until I heard the words "hey Boo." That was a girlfriend of a cousin of mine who recognized me. She took me under her wing, introduced me to the crew, and then I turned into a different person. Being in school was now fun; I was on the Step Team with a bunch of amazing ladies. We would all sit together at lunch and laugh and sing. Shoot, we would even have a photoshoot at times. No one knew my pain under so many layers, and that was alright. When I was with them, I didn't have to think about them because we'd always be laughing having such a good time. However, when I was not around them, I was a different person, very quiet and timid. I was scared to say anything, even though I had so much to say. They used to think I had some sort of mute disorder. It made me think I had it myself as well, shoo! After so long.

One of my teachers referred me to a counselor at the school. They wanted to know what was going on and if they could do anything to help. I didn't have the words to explain to someone I didn't believe wanted to help me. They are just doing their job if you ask me. Shantel talked to some folks like that, and where did it get her? It got her in a place that considered her a danger. As I said, the system doesn't love girls that look like us. As they continued to ask me repeatedly and weekly, calling me down to the office, I sat there, letting the concerned voice go in one ear and out the other. I guess I was just so fed up with the constant visits that I had let out a sarcastic voice tone saying, "Find my Birth Mama, that is what you can do." Demanding an impossible action, thinking I would keep them busy didn't go as planned.

The next week I got called in the office, and there was a man on the phone saying, "Desiray, I got your Mother on."

"Could this be happening? Was this a dream, a sick joke, or some figment of my imagination?"

I was quiet. Suddenly, on the other end of the phone I felt and Kool-Aid smile from ear to ear, smiling at me before I heard anything.

Then there it was, "Hey, Dee Dee," she said.

I smiled, and I replied, "Hey, Ma."

CHAPTER 3
I Imagine Myself

My first real job was doing housekeeping at 15-years-old at the Ramada Inn. Early I learned how to budget to buy the things I needed. I was already living in the real world. So, I had money. I quickly told my Granny and other family members the news. "I found my Mama" It spread like wildfire. My Daddy found out; you better believe he tracked me down and forbids me from meeting her. He told me; it was just going to open old wounds. I wanted to know for who? I was far from healed. My wounds were wide open, feeling the pain daily. I had just learned to live with them. At the end of the day, I was determined that no one could tell me anything. I felt like I was on my own; had my own money, so I did what I wanted.

I went to the Greyhound Station, got myself a ticket, and went to Chicago, Illinois, to meet my Mama. The six-hour ride had me sleeping off and on. As I slept, I dreamed of how this meeting would go.

"I stepped off the bus, and she ran to swoop me up. She kissed me so tight and told me how she has dreamed of this day. We drove all around the city as she showed me all her favorite spots. We sat and shared a hot meal she cooked for me as my taste buds celebrated after each bite. There we were sitting under the stars talking about everything."

I woke up by the driver saying, "Welcome to Chicago, Illinois folks."

I got up then fear took over me. I tried to turn away and walk back to my seat, but a line behind me was full of folks staring at me like angry bulls. Therefore, to avoid conflict, I just tiptoed on out the door. As I placed my feet on solid ground, I saw a round-shaped caramel complexed lady, wearing a black t-shirt and some black leggings running towards me. Her Tennis shoes flickered in the night as they jogged to me. She had her hair sleeked up into a tight ponytail, and then I heard a voice say, "Dee Dee!"

"This was my Mama?" I thought.

We hugged, and then she said, "Give me your bag, the bus about to be here."

I was quiet, and I just followed her. We waited a good two minutes for the bus. Then we boarded as she paid both our fares. Walking to the very end of the bus, she let out a sigh and said, "I know you got some questions for me. I am ready!"

My very first question was, "What happened to my sister Jazzman? How was she killed?" I saw a look of terror take over her face as she began telling the story.

"I left you and your sister with him. All I did was run to the store to get him some cigarettes. I came back, and y'all were sleeping on the couch. I woke up Jazzman and bathed her, then laid her on the bed. When I woke up, she was gone."

In my head, I thought, *"That is not what you said under oath in court. I got the newspaper clippings that I'd be happy to break out Boo Boo."* Instead, I just grew silent, having absolutely nothing to say in return. We sat there in silence for a while until she broke the peace.

"Next question?"

"Why didn't you come to find us?" I asked.

She gonna say, "Cause I knew y'all would find me when you got ready. Soon your little brother Glyn and sister Tyyonna will reach out to find me too."

I was growing irritated by her answers and not able to find words to express them. I turned my head to the window, falling into a deep stare as her voice faded out like a loud ringing in my ear.

"Dee Dee!" she snapped at me, "come on Baby."

I followed her down the street to this stairway leading into the basement. She had an area all fixed up for me. She begins to talk about who was all coming to see me. Each time she spoke, I unintentionally zoned her out. All I could do was stare at her. I was trying my best to make my last dream match up to my reality. I met so many different people who all seemed to know me and claimed to have missed me so much. Yet, none of them missed me enough to reach out to me or find me to let me know they indeed missed me.

The next day we were back on the bus headed to meet my Grandma Faye. She asked, "You hungry, Baby?"

I replied, "Yes," so eagerly excited to eat a meal that I wouldn't forget. She pulled out a TV dinner, and I sat on the chair in total silence. My mind couldn't wrap itself around what was going on. Was this my family? The people who I thought were the missing piece of my puzzle. Why couldn't I get what I wanted? I knew better that life didn't work that way. I just wrote Imagined Myself!

"IMAGINE MYSELF"

Though Some Things may get me Down,
I find Strength WITHIN MYSELF
And try NOT to Frown

Yes, my Heart is FILLED with so much Pain,
But I take I take a Deep Breath,
"IMAGINE MYSELF"
So, I'm Calm and don't go Insane

My Jesus knows just what to Say
When I Bow My Knees,
And begin to Pray

"I IMAGINE MYSELF"
So, life's One Big Party!

My family is together AT LAST, Cool,
Now I don't have to tell anyone
To KISS MY A**!

Only because. . .

"I IMAGINE MYSELF!"

Sitting in a place with No Insecurities

Now, I'm FINALLY Happy!

Only because. . .

"I IMAGINE MYSELF!"

Instead of Love Fading Away

"I IMAGINE MYSELF"

So, it NEVER goes away

The sun was shining through my Grandma's thin curtains, so warm and cozy on my face. I wasn't even looking forward to breakfast, so I immediately began gathering my things ready to head back to Sunnyvale, W.I. The Greyhound ride was too so fast. I took a nap to sort my thoughts and was waking up to the driver announcing our arrival. I was ready to face the "I told you so" from my Daddy. But he just had a look on his face of relief that I had made it back. I knew that joker loved me; he just hasn't learned how to show it!

Getting asked how it was; left me feeling so uneasy. My feelings hadn't come to the surface yet. So, my answer to them all was a question, "It was alright." Honestly, I just wanted to curl up like a ball into my Mommy's (Taylor) arms for a good cry. Since we were in two different states, that wasn't an option. So, I kept on keeping on.

CHAPTER 4
TRE

Up until now, I have been lost. I love just because it feels good. You know what I mean. Do you care for someone, expecting nothing in return strictly because it's the right thing to do! I did feel that love back in return from my Granny, Tee Tee, Bestie, and my cousin Teddy. My Granny was such a soft and sweet, beautiful Black Queen. She treasured the Lord, but you bet not try her. She loved me so much. I remember being maybe three or 4-years-old Shantel and I were in her Chicago apartment being spoiled. We had just finished eating something with some sauce on it. There I was, playing hide and seek with my cousins, and ended up in Granny's closet. I wiped my hands all over her pretty white coat and ran out. To this day, I remembered how I shed those big ol' crocodile tears, crying out, "I didn't do it!" and just like that, Granny said, "My Baby didn't do that," it was the most fun, loving thing Granny ever did for me. She knew I did it. But the fact that I was upset about it made her make it all go away. You see, that is the Granny I have, one who loves me unconditionally.

Today is June 28, 2014, and it's my last day in Sunnyvale, W.I. As I sit here in tears, all I wish for is my Daddy to walk through the door. A few days ago, we had an awful debate over me leaving Sunnyvale. Him in tears vs. My "I don't give a damn" look. I just wanted him to say as his last words to me, "be safe, Baby girl, and I love you!"

Instead, he said, "If you think going over a thousand miles away gone make you happy, you wrong!"

What killed me was the tears he shed, yelling at me, "I may not have been the best husband, but I am a damn good Daddy!"

As he kept talking, the look on my face grew even bolder! He read it well too.

As it said, *"You think buying us Christmas gifts and paying a few of my bills counts as being a good Daddy? You never came to any of my milestones, never told me how proud you were of me. But he was quick to call me all out my name! Now you have the nerve to pout. We had a relationship because I longed for a Daddy. A real Daddy! He would come through for me if I were doing everything; he said the way he said it. The moment I tried to live my own life, the second I disobeyed him, I wasn't his daughter. He would be so furious with me that he'd ride past us walking and keep going. How can you call that a damn good daddy? No matter how much my Pappi drifts away and disobeys me. He will always be my son. I'll always be his mother. I understand being upset with each other, but when he would say those words to me, disowning me for whatever reason. I would disconnect from him even more. But here he was crying a river because I decided to leave it all behind. Why? I thought. Was it because you won't be able to hurt me in any way anymore? Because you won't be able to control me anymore."*

But all I ended was saying was, "We are leaving, I've made my mind up!"

He started to say something, but he must have noticed the *"I don't give a damn"* look on my face. Because instead, he just shook his head and slammed my door.

As Pappi played in the yard that he has grown to love for the last four years, one last time. Tears began to stream down my ashy hot face. I touched my face as if I had a fever, all it was, was my body temperature rising from so many tears of fear.

I begin to cry out to God, "Please, Lord, guide me, take away all things and make me new. Please, Lord, settle in my spirit!"

As I patted my face dry, walks in one of my best cousins, Teddy. She was the only person in this world who knew me inside and out. We would always sit and talk about this, that, and the other. She was so amazing at just listing. We embraced each other so tight. As tears rolled to the back of my throat, I told myself to get it together. I couldn't let her know that I was so scared of what my future held. I couldn't tell her that as much as she wanted me to stay, I too wanted to go right back into my beautiful home full of memories and sleep it all off. But I needed to go, I just did! It came time to tell my Tee Tee Goodbye; it was the hardest. Tee Tee was my Dad's twin sister. She really should have been my mama. We are so much alike, from the looks on down to the personalities sweet but super feisty. She has one daughter, Nika, and I are a year apart. We all look like triplets, I tell you. When they did ask, how's your mama and sister doing? I knew they were talking about these two.

When I got my hug from Tee Tee, oh, she cried like a baby. It was so refreshing to see that she didn't mind showing she was going to miss us. In return, I let mine show as I let out the knot unravel in the back of my throat. My tears quietly streamed down my face as we intercepted love. I collected myself and surprised her with a huge canvas of Pappi and me. Our smiles will light up her living room for sure.

"Any time you get to missing us, just look on over at us, Tee Tee," I told her. That made her croquet smile appear.

Nika walked past our picture and said, "What's up?" We broke out in laughter, making the air a bit easier to take in.

Then there was my big sister, a few days beforehand I had a small going away party. I gave away so much. No sense in letting it all go to waste.

I asked if she needed anything else.

She replied, "All I want is for you and my nephew not to leave."

In return, I said, "I'll see what I can do."

She said, "I'm sure it's a laugh out loud behind that." I noticed her distraught matter and did not even bother to respond.

Like really? What was I gonna say?

When Kingston, my nephew, gave Pappi his hug, he told Pappi, "You're going to Texas, and I'm going to miss you because you're my best bud, right?" Pappi shook his head in confusion, and the knot in my throat came back as if it never left.

I thought, *"I am taking my son from the only life he knows. Who will he play with? What will bring a smile to his face the way his cousin Kingston does? Best cousins since day one separated because of me. I felt so horrible."*

However, as I packed the last of our things in the car. My heart still longed for that empty hole to be filled. True, all my family and friends are here. But I knew we deserved better than this life we had been living.

After the police shot Tre 14 times for sleeping in the park, a very dear man to my heart, a man who would die for me 14 times for sleeping in the park, that was the icing on the cake. I was ready to leave! You see, Tre and I use to date. He loved my dirty draws, you hear me. However, he was sick and just not aware of it. He would hear voices and pick with my Pappi. I remember Pappi was sleeping in the bed with us, and I accidentally kicked him.

He jumped up out the bed, yelling, "I told you he was evil; he out to get me!" It was things like that that threw me off, but he meant no harm.

He would move the world for me; for Pappi, I can bet you that for anyone he loved. The way his mind was set up, I would not take a chance and allow him to hurt my son. We moved to just being best of friends, although he still tried to get me back in all he did, I wasn't going. I would sometimes let the phone ring when he called because it was always the same ol' same; him pouring out his love for me. It's sad how Mental Health awareness is overlooked in the Black community, especially for our Black males. Tre would always do off the wall things and when I asked him the reason why. He would say the voices told me to. Man, he was the sweetest man I had ever met. I loved him! Memories of him haunted me. I was so used to answering the phone for him when I wanted. He had to call me at least ten times a day, no exaggeration. Time had gone by, and I hadn't talked to him for almost a month. That was totally unlike him; he called to tell me he loves us daily. I reached out to him time and time again and couldn't get through. I figured maybe he had found someone to love him the way he deserved to be loved. Someone who didn't see him as an option, I never imagined how much I would miss his calls. I took him for granted and was feeling some kind of way about it. But I took it as my loss and wished him well in my mind.

My 24th birthday hit; I had just come back from the piercing place getting my belly button pierced. I was sipping on some wine, feeling myself. My phone kept going off.

"Who was I was getting a call from?"

I answered, and there was my bestie on the other end asking me, "Dezy, is Tre dead?" I was thrown for a loop.

I screamed, "What! Not my Tre!" my heart began to race, then I said, "let me find out, Girl, and call you back."

So, I looked it up, and before I knew it, I was on the floor. The newspaper said he was shot 14 times because a Starbucks racist employee called the cops on him. Apparently, he was sleeping in the park near the Starbucks when a police officer killed him. His funeral had come and gone 36 days prior.

"Why tho?" Is all I thought, and the guilt ate at me, *"Should I have stayed with him? Maybe if he wouldn't have been at the park if my heart were more inviting. Maybe I could have tried harder to convince him to see a doctor? Maybe I could have saved his life but looked the other way for my own selfish reasons. Just maybe?"*

I wanted to leave Wisconsin to run away from it all. Runaway from all the things and people hindering my growth. But all I could do was write.

"TRE"

To a Man who Loved me,
A Man who Adored me

Why Oh Why?
Did that sickness have to take you away from me?
We always Agreed to Disagree,
That you ALWAYS left up to me

My way was the Only Way you'd say
Never leaving room for Dismay

I couldn't make you Mad Enough,
I couldn't make you Sad Enough
You loved the Hell out of me,
Still, I played it Tough

The enemy attacked you at your Lowest Point
Misconstrued by the Voices,
It pulled you down to the dirt

I'm a King you'd say!
STONE MACHO all day!
Still all you wanted was for
Me to Lead the way

Thinking of the Last Night I seen you.
How you kissed my Lips, held my face
Your eyes, Oh your Eyes
Touched my Heart with such an Embrace
I MELTED!

Never thinking we'd be a part due to such a cause
Truly that Sickness took you away
Long before that Cop shot you Dead
In such a Horrible way

Night fell upon me, I grew Weak
There came the enemy Attacking me
My Soul had developed and Unexplained Hole

What more could have said,

Surly there was MORE I could have Done

The enemy began to Play the Blame Game,

Falling for his Tricks,

Confused, I became Calling out

Only my own Name

O God, My God. Sorry for what I have done!

Tre, my Darling Tre,

Forgive me for what I could have done

My Heart is Broken and Filled with so much Pain,

Yet, I know my Father will NEVER Forsake me

Or Leave me in Vain

I Flashback in time for a while,

Before I know it, I begin to Smile

Thank you, Tre

For showing me the Way

The Real Meaning of Unconditional Love

I SAY!

Picturing you Gazing Down at me

From Heaven above,

Letting go of what "I THINK" I could have done

No one can Top

How or What you Do

From the Bottom of my Heart,

I LOVE YOU!

R.I.P. Yours Truly!

CHAPTER 5
Let's Go Back

As I watched all my furniture sit on my front lawn. Cars stopped one by one taking what they wanted.

I drifted off into thought, *"Why was I leaving my beautiful home that my son had spent his entire life? Why was I giving away all my nice furniture to strangers? Why was I leaving the highest paying job I ever had? Like Fa'real, why in the Hell was I leaving all I know? Family, friends, MY LIFE?"*

Then I heard a voice say as loud as can be, "Because life waits on nobody!" that voice was mine! It was right!

Another day here in Sunnyvale, WI. would mean another day of disappointment, loneliness, and abuse in all forms. Staying here meant me settling. Settling for a less life than I know my Pappi and I deserved. I quickly shook off my regrets. We got in my little old Grey 96 Honda Accord and started it up. As I pulled off, I looked in the rear-view mirror at my past, shed a rainfall of tears as we got on down the road heading to FORT WORTH, TX!

It's funny cause I use to wonder why I was like the way I was. I loved just to love. I give because it feels good. Even if I give my all doing so, it is just a rewarding feeling. That feeling is enough for me in this lifetime to make a difference in this world. So, I have to keep pushing until I am surrounded by folks who allow me to grow into that me! People like Pappi Aunties in Milwaukee they were the bomb.com. Well, they were not his blood Aunties; they were Johnny's siblings. Johnny! My 1st love, he seemed to be all I ever needed.

I was with the girls from school, hanging out at the Boys and Girls Club. A slinky, light-skinned thing came up talking to me; I don't even recall what he said. Just the fact that he approached me got me all in an uproar. That night we ran all my minutes down out of my Nokia phone. He said all the right things my vulnerable heart needed to hear. I was sold! You could not tell me he and I were not going to spend forever together; I just knew it. He was not quick to sleep with me after that conversation. Even when I was trying to keep up with the crowd, he kept telling me I wasn't ready. He told me his deepest darkest secrets. We would lay up all night just talking. Most of the time, I was just listening. I enjoyed him opening up to me. He loved me; I could tell.

One night as we were lying there at his Auntie's house on the couch, he said, "I have something to tell you, but don't get mad."

"What?" I asked.

"You was a bet," he said softly, and looking puzzled, he repeated it, "they bet me that I couldn't get you."

"But we didn't have sex yet," I said.

"Exactly, that's how you know I care." I felt special.

This was gonna be my forever guy; he made me so happy. Then, something happened, but I don't know what happened; it did so very fast. He became no good for me; truly a typical 17-year-old boy. Like seriously, what was I thinking? He did me so dirty, from cheating on me, fighting on me, to just not givin' a damn about me. But a young girl born into abuse lived in abuse and raising herself since she was a freshman in high school knew nothing else.

One day we were in my very first apartment. I had just had my 17th

birthday, and he was 18. I had a terrible attitude, just sick of his shit. Not sick enough to leave, apparently. He had his older brother over and I remember him pulling me into the bathroom and choking my life.

He got in my face telling me through his teeth, "Chill out, do you understand me?"

In my head, I thought, *"You the one cheating on me and talking about it so casually like my feeling don't matter."* But instead, I was excited, ready to take a stand.

He tried to exit quickly back to his brother as if nothing happened. My blood pressure flew up so high. I remember catching him by surprise as I started pulling him back into the small 6 by 6 feet bathroom, kicking and punching. I didn't utter a word out my mouth, just allowed all my feelings to come out in a ballistic way. Before I knew it, we were bursting open the door fighting all into the studio apartment. Front and center, we were entertainment for his company that watched with pleasure. His long arms reached out, striking me as hard as he could in my face. Left, Right, Right, Left, repeatedly.

Finally, his brother broke us up. Johnny walked outside, his brother followed, and they were gone for a while. I locked myself in the bathroom, quietly breaking down in tears. The hot water let off so much steam as it drowned out my cries. I didn't even know why I was crying. I guess there were so many reasons my brain cells couldn't pick one. So, I just sat there until my body grew weak to sleep; I went hoping the tears would soon stop flowing. Later that night, my body began to feel all the pain. I played it off, not wanting an ounce of sympathy from neither of them. What I did get was a compliment.

"You were eating them punches up, wasn't you Dez?"

Feeling like that was a good thing, I gave a satisfying smile saying back to him, "You better know it."

As time went on, we never really broke up, if that makes any sense. Eventually, he moved down the street from me with another girl. I turned into an abusive addictive stalker. I needed him to be okay, even though I was far from okay when I was with him. I experienced health problems that I didn't take seriously because I was too busy wondering if he came to my apartment and I wasn't there, I would miss him. He and the abuse were all I knew.

I am sitting up listing to some Betty in my apartment all I alone.

I got to thinking, *"I must have been born in the wrong decade. Because all I ever wondered was how it was to live back then? I used to swear what I was searching for is how it use to be in the old days."*

Full of LOVE, I wanted to go back! Back to then, but of course, all I could do was write."

"LET'S GO BACK"

LET'S GO BACK
BACK to Then, to Remember When

When we Laughed just because we could
No If, Ands or I wish I Woulds

We just Did it, we just Lived it
LET'S GO BACK, BACK, WAY BACK,
To Love, just like the One from Above

When you didn't Feel Weak
Or Ashamed to Cry,
Because there was ALWAYS someone there
To Dry Your Eyes

Come on, I'm Ready to Go
Shit, I'll even Beat you to the Door
We are Out of Here,
Don't nobody got time for Fear

We are going BACK to Laugh, to Love, to Live!

See where I am going folks Live to Give,

They Love JUST BECAUSE they can.

And Baby Please, they are NOT WORRIED about you,

But their Own Man.

SEE I AM GOING BACK

You can Stay Here if you want to,

And Live in Lack

But me Myself

OH, I GOTS TO GO BACK

Where there was No Such Thing

As children Growing up in such a Huge Race,

They were Content with Staying in their Place

Goodbye, Sayonara, So Long, Adios Duce-Duce

Your Invitation has been Given

Now the Question is…

ARE YOU WILLING?

Yes or No is the Question,

All I can say is

Please DON'T Miss Out

ON THIS BLESSING

Whether you Choose to Stay or Go,

I don't know

But I'll Holla cause I am Out the Door

HEADED BACK, BACK, BACK

To a place Designed,

WITH ME IN MIND!

You Coming?

WELCOME TO YOUR PEACE OF MIND!

CHAPTER 6

Fork in My Path

I had finally turned 18 and had purchased my 1st car, a white Buick Century. I had no idea how to drive, but I was tired of catching the bus to work, wash clothes, and going to the grocery store. I worked at this great school as a teacher's aide since my junior year in high school, which allowed me to save money easily. I never longed for much; that was just me.

One day Johnny had my car and was supposed to pick me up from work. That day my stomach was hurting so bad, my blood pressure was up, and I was severely fatigued. I was horrible at taking care of myself. All I wanted to do was go home and sleep. I was glad Johnny was picking me up because I was in no condition to drive. But, oh how he had to be the ass that was staring me in my face every day. He never showed; I ended up catching the bus and knew exactly where he was. I marched right on over there to the girl's apartment. Oh, I was livid! Just as I was running up, there they were getting out of my damn car, the damn car that I worked my tail off to get. She said something to me, and before I knew it, we were fighting. I looked around, ready to give Johnny some too. But that joker runs into the apartment. I bet we had stroked his ego really well as he watched from the window. After I had her on the ground, I jumped up, got in my car, and zoomed off. I must've run over a few curves and cats because it was a really loud and bumpy ride back up the street to my apartment. That day I learned how to drive! Even after that, I would not leave him alone. He came to my door, and there I was, arms wide open.

The very 1st time I called myself trying to move on, this man and his brother came to my apartment and jumped the guy. We laid there so in love as if nothing happened.

In the back of my mind, I thought, *"Why Desiray, why?"*

I was lost in the moment; I knew it wasn't going to last long. But it felt so good I pushed all the red flags out the way and enjoyed it while I could! A fake love that never felt so good. PURE TOXIC!

Years went by then I finally decided to date another guy. I got pregnant and had my son Pappi. Pappi came right on time; I was so alone and felt like each day I awoke with a purpose. You couldn't tell me nothing about Pappi. I was a young mother who was going to make sure this young man grew up to be totally different from Johnny. It felt good to be needed and loved, just because! My Pappi gave me purpose and became my entire world! However, that was nothing but a pebble in my path right back into Johnny's nest. I never left Johnny alone; he never left me alone. That alone is what made me think I was "It."

"He can't leave me alone, so he must love me," I'd say each time trying to convince my conscience I was alright.

Little did I know I was not "IT," I was just a fool.

As my Granny used to say, "You see a fool, bump her head!"

Guess I wasn't getting enough headaches because now I wasn't sure who the father was. Of course, I wanted it to be Johnny's. But I had learned a long time ago; I don't ever get what I want.

The day I found out Pappi wasn't his, I was hurt and relieved at the same time. I told myself nothing was tying me to him now. I could leave him alone and get my life together with his birth father and be happy! Then his biological father wanted no parts of my son. There I went, running back to what I knew. Even though Pappi was not his, his family claimed him, as did Johnny. Back under his spell, the abuse continued. I settled for some low shit; do you hear me.

One day I was going to the laundry mat to wash all our things. Johnny assured me he was going to watch him. He even told me to take my time to give me a little break. Pappi was about three months and sleeping so soundly on the bed. I get to the laundry mat about three blocks down the road and realized I had left my money I needed to wash our clothes. When I got back to my house, this man was nowhere in sight. He had taken my money, left the door wide open, and their pappi were all alone on the bed crying his eyes out. Can you believe I allowed this sucka to come back two days later? He knew I would and played on my emotions every time. I told myself I was doing it for Pappi to keep him in his life. The truth was I didn't know my worth. I was immune to the hurt, to the pain! He would treat me like the lowest of the lows one minute, then the next we were all good. My attitude was out of this world. Something in me kept trying to burst out, to tell itself.

"You are not this person."

"This is not you."

But I never allowed it to fully surface. Anytime he would do something disrespectful, I'd get so petty. I'd do things like unplugging the TV in the middle of his game. You know, feeling like I am standing up for myself. We'd fight like wild animals. He didn't care that I was a young lady. I didn't care that I was just a young lady as well. I'd fight back as if I could whoop that 6'1 inch, 180-pound man. My whole 4'11 inches, 100-pounds was convinced in the midst of fist swinging. He'd always get the best of me, but you better believe I wasn't going down without a fight.

I was just a young lady. A naïve young lady who he claimed he loved that he'd do anything for me! I allowed all that to happen.

For eight years, I was on hold. My life, my worth, my peace! TRUE HAPPINESS! If I called myself moving on to a new relationship, Johnny was right on the other end of that. If he called himself trying to move on to a new relationship. I was right on the other side of that! TOXIC!

Johnny had one too many tickets and eventually put in jail. Not much of a difference as he was inside; I still was there. The thing was, he had gotten out of jail, and I didn't even know it. Here I am thinking when he gets out, we are gonna do this, that, and the other. To my surprise, he had those plans already with another girl. I had to find out via social media as I scrolled through seeing him posing with another girl. My heart broke all over again as reality hit me. I knew he would be at my door tomorrow, and I knew I would welcome him as if he never left. I was okay with such horrible emotional abuse. It was just like a constant circle that I had to exit. Even though I was hurt, I was relieved as well. This feeling made me even more eager to get our final hugs from his aunties in Milwaukee, W.I., and keep it moving to our fresh start. True, I felt ashamed of all the years I had wasted. I came to that fork in the path and took the wrong turn; shame on me. As always, all I could do was write.

"FORK IN THE PATH"

Which way do I Go?

No one seems to Know

There is a

FORK IN MY PATH

Left, Right, Straight, or Back?

Which way do I Go?

As I turned Left

Towards the Crooked Arrow

I looked up and suddenly,

The Sky begins to Sink Low

Not a ray of Sunshine in Sight,

Just Dozens and Dozens of Clouds

Putting up a Fight

Mountains of Stone, Piled up

One after another in my Path

I am tired of Fighting

Let me just Lay in Fear for awhile

They say it's Okay to Fall,

Just as Long as you Get Back Up

So, I Stand up, Pushing on

With the oz. of Strength Remaining.

Weak from weathering the Storm, Sleet, and Snow

I CRIED OUT,

PLEASE, GOD, I CAN'T TAKE NO MORE!

Shame on me for allowing it

To reach this Far,

Now I am Walking Around

Trying to Heal from all these Scars

Push the Sun through the Clouds

Knock the Mountains down out of my Path

Hold my Hand as I Travel

This Strenuous Journey

You have my Word

I Vow to NEVER go alone Anymore.

Thank you, My God,
The next time I reach
A FORK IN MY PATH,
I'll remember God's Wrath.

I'll seek FIRST the Kingdom of Heaven
So, everything will Line Up.

In Your Name' I Pray
Amen!

CHAPTER 7

I'm Blessed

As I got down on the highway, I heard my best friend's voice echo in my head! *"You are so Brave!"* although I felt like a selfish coward. I let her words manifest in my heart and kept on driving! Sally has been my BFF (Best Friend Forever) since the 9th grade. She has seen me at my absolute worst, and I've seen her at hers. Yet, we never strayed apart for too long. When we were in gym class and I would always have candy and gum. One day she asked for some and I gave it to her. And from that moment on, we have been joined at the hip. I remember nights I had no idea where I was going to sleep. Her house was it. Ms. Lucy Smith is what I would call her mother. She has a heart made out of gold. She didn't know me from Adam or Eve. But always welcomed me into her heart, into her life, and into her home with pleasure. I was loved by them, just because for sure. Mann, staying up half the night just talking, laughing, and listening to music was it. I tell you. For a second, all my troubles melted away any time I was in their presence.

With a du-rag on my nappy head, basketball shorts on my frail legs, and a thin tank top covering my chest. I drove, drove, and drove as Mary Mary played in the background, *"GO GET IT, GO GET, GO GET YOUR BLESSING."* It pumped me up a bit as I kept talking to the Lord, only asking Him to guide me and protect us along the way. We were rolling, and Pappi had his games that I had downloaded onto my laptop. He was being such a big boy. I had my music, and I was A-okay.

It begins to pour down outside like cats and dogs. It made my body so limp, but I just kept on driving. For a hot second, I drifted off in thought, reflecting on the saying, *"When it rains, God is crying? Did I make God cry? If I did, what kind of tears were they? Were the Lord shedding tears of joy for me? Or tears of sadness for me? All I ever wanted to do was please Him! I know I had failed at that in the past, but I was determined to make it right."*

I was on edge a bit, seared from the heat coming from the sky as we continued South. It's now a new day, and my body began to shut down. I prayed for the Lord to let us make it to a rest stop. I was exhausted, hungry from giving Pappi all the snacks, and needed to stop. Just when I felt my eyes closing, I heard the GPS say welcome to Kansas! The truck stop was off to the right, and I pulled in with relief. Both of us asleep in the front seat; it was so uncomfortable. I kept peeking out the window, but all I saw was the dark sky hovering over us. I was so scared; I couldn't sleep much at first. My mind just wouldn't turn off like a bad record skipping repeatedly. I had to get some sort of sleep if I was going to drive again. I clung to my faith and went fast to sleep. I was dreaming about our fresh start!

As the sun awoke us, I fed Pappi the last sandwich we had left. He ate so quickly as his eyeballs smiled at a playground. Out we climbed bodies so stiff. We played like two big ol' kids for 30 minutes or so. My Granny called to check in with me and I remember her and my Grand Dad being so proud of me for making it thus far.

"Dez, you are a phenomenal woman," they told me.

I locked those words in my soul as we made our way to Texas. No longer did I feel sadness or regret. Instead, I was excited, knowing I'll get a chance to be me! Living a life WE deserve! One where we will be living our life to the fullest each day as we walk in our purpose. WE deserved all the desires of our heart and we were going to get it for sure! I knew that way down deep in my soul.

Here it is June 30th, 2014, and here we are crossing the line to TEXAS! I pulled up to the Dirt Motel I quickly picked up the key. I put Pappi in front of the TV and ran to the shower! It was the best shower I have had in my Life! Do you hear me? I didn't think at all. I just relaxed my mind and enjoyed the soapy suds falling from my body. It was so much to take in! I heard a voice yell: I did it! I made it! All the way from Sunnyvale, W.I. To Fort Worth, TX! That voice was me and it was right too. I was proud of myself and to show myself appreciation. Honey, I got cute, fixed up my Pappi, and we were out exploring. We found a park. It was blistering hot out. Something we hadn't felt ever. But we didn't trip. We played like two kids who had been held hostage for years. We were finally free! Free to grow into the individuals God called us to be ready. Looking in the future, no more in the past, there was absolutely nothing there for us!

Ninety days later, trying to get a job was the hardest; all I ever wanted to do was teach. But it seems as if the TV my Daddy gave to me was on my record as me stealing it from him? What in the world? Frustrated at that, I decided I will not let my past hinder me from laying it to rest.

Trying to get ready for the next day was the worst. Roaches swarmed the room; we were knocking them off just to sleep. Then my phone rang. It was Granny!

All I heard was tears, "What's wrong, Granny?" I asked.

"Brian is dead?"

"What in the World, Granny?!" I screamed!

"Yes, Baby!" she said, confirming this nightmare.

I asked what happened? She couldn't quite get it out. It was something about in the shower, heart hurting, and him dying right in her arms. We cried together as I remembered his last words to me.

"Dez, you are a Phenomenal Woman," Shantel called me to check on me.

She knows how my anxiety and depression get. It was nice to hear a sense of concern in her voice even though she appeared to be the toughest of the tough. I knew my sister; she was hard on the outside yet soft and squishy on the inside. Especially for the folks, she loves. She passed the phone to Teddy, and we talked. She told me my Daddy was there. I asked her to give him the phone. We hadn't spoken since we last got into it. I had no clue what to say. But after my Grand Dad was taken away so suddenly, I had to say something to him.

With tears blocking my voice box, I finally manage to squeeze out, "Daddy, I just wanted to talk to you."

He goes, "I am listening."

I said, "I just wanted to tell you I love you."

I heard a burst of tears from the other end of the phone before he replied, "I love you too." I hung up feeling so sad.

I knew I wasn't going to make it to his funeral. All I wanted to do was sleep. So, I did as the tears soaked my pillow. I was determined to find a job. I had so many interviews, but nothing concrete. I would have to take Pappi with me to each one, leave the car on high air, and pray it all worked out. The last interview I had, I just knew I had it in the bag, then I came out to a flat tire with absolutely no tools. There I was embarrassed that these folks have seen me leave my child out in the car. I knew for sure that job was a wrap! They did lend a hand and wished me luck. One thing for sure, I thank God for blessing me with this little boy. Some nights all he had was a bag of potato chips to eat, and he did not complain, not once. I just kept telling him to be grateful that we had each other. Some folks were out here with no one. He understood, and he watched me closely. So, I always wore a smile of gratitude, even though half the time it was forced. Though the road was rough, each morning when we woke, Pappi and I would say, "We're blessed."

"I'M BLESSED"

24 years later, I'm still here

Simply because I've always held God near

Been beaten down to the Ground

Even though I wore Constant Frowns

I'M BLESSED

Worried about This or That

Please, I am Learning that

MY GOD LOVES ME JUST LIKE THAT!

I'M BLESSED

Heartache, Heartbreak one after another

Prayed that God would send me a King

Tired of these "Common Things."

Hush My Child

YOU'RE BLESSED

It is One Thing after Another
Nothing seems to go Right
Such a Tiring Fight

Yet here I Stand in the Ring
I hear them Singing
SHE'S BLESSED!

CHAPTER 8

God Got Me!

Pappi would sit up and play games on the laptop and listen to music. Then as the pictures slid past of our old life, he cried! He wouldn't say a word; just stare and cry. When I asked him if he wanted to talk about it, he cried out in such a panic.

"I miss Kingston, my room, and everybody in Sunnyvale."

It sounded as if he was going to hyperventilate. So, there was no need for me to say anything in return. I knew what he was feeling, I too missed the comfort we had no matter what pain came with it. I just held him and my tears so tightly to my heart. On the other hand, Texas for me was peaceful; despite the condition we were living. I had nothing or no one hindering me from being this free. I missed my family dearly, but I just kept telling myself if you want better, you must be better. My goal is to better myself through God's eyes. I want to wake up each day with purpose, walk in it, and then when I lay my head to rest, I am able to do so with a sense of satisfaction. Just knowing I was able to be me and to love just because I can!

Money was at its end just when I figured things were getting better. No luck! We got the boot of out the room we were living in. Pappi and I were now on the street, hungry and all alone. I thought back to the rain we experienced on our drive to Texas and muttered quietly to myself, "Oh, those must have been sad tears the Lord shaded for me."

After 62 long days, I had had it! Back to Sunnyvale, we go. The tiredness, feeling of failure, and terrified of what was to come next ran me back to the door I had just came from. That door of abuse! That door of settling, that horrible door of hindering because I knew there was no way I would prosper in that place. The crazy thing is as I traveled down the road, my car engine burned out. As I watched the smoke arise from it, I heard the Lord say, "I GOT YOU!" With tears in my eyes, I had to be strong for Pappi. I grabbed a pen and paper to calm my nerves. I heard the Lord's voice again. I said to myself, "*God got me!*

"GOD GOT ME"

When the Sun hides itself
And the Stars shine bright
My Mind begins to Wonder
Off unto the Moonlight

At the Peak of my Breaking Point
My God drops His Arms around me
As my Soul Breaks

Why do you Weep my child?
Why do you insist on allowing such Foolishness
To Consume you?
For you know I am no such Author of it

Suddenly, I became Lighter
The Fear, Frustration, Worries
All of the Enemies Whispers
Began to Roll of me like Sweat

HE WHISPERED ONCE MORE
I GOT YOU!!

As I Drifted off upon a cloud Full of Dreams
Glorious rays of Sunshine awoke me

I felt myself getting Weary
There was His Voice again saying,
O' YE' OF LITTLE FAITH
I GOT YOU

I Stood up with such Great Poise
A New Look appeared on my Face
My Walk became a Strut
FULL OF I GOT THIS AND THAT!

Combined with a Load of Confidence,
You couldn't help but Smile at
I looked all my obstacles dead in the face and said,
BABY BYE! GOD GOT ME!

I kept calling shelters, determined to get in one and Boom! We were in luck; they had just got an opening. Thank you, God! We were warm, fed, and feeling alright. The shelter really helped us. We had our own room, comfy separate beds, and the food was good. For the first week, I kept Pappi busy with what he loves to do. He enjoyed the games on the laptop, constant movies on TV, and all. We didn't go out; we just stayed in our room. I didn't want to get to know anyone. I was seriously disgusted with our entire situation. I felt like such a failure for my Pappi. He was watching me, and I kept telling myself to get it together. Lord knows I was trying to. I was blessed with a little boy like him. He would cry every now in then when he thought about Sunnyvale, W.I. But, besides that. He was holding up, being grateful for what we do have. I would catch him staring at me, giving me looks of Love. How can he still love me after I got us in this situation? I would wonder day in and out if he would resent me as he got older. Days flew by and there he was, still giving me that "Look of Love."

Trying to keep my Pappi happy, we were back exploring. I found another park and let him go at it. But this time just watching him, sucking up all his 4-year-old happy squeals and excitement. I let him play until it was time for dinner at the shelter. Then we headed back only to get lost. All I kept thinking was we are going to miss curfew and get kicked out. We were going to be back on the street. How could I do this to Pappi? Before I knew it, my body began to freeze up; fear took over. All the air seemed to escape from my lung's seconds at a time. Squabbling for air, I told Pappi. "Call 911!" waiting for the ambulance to come, I prayed. As the words escaped my mouth ever so loudly, I heard a voice echoing my words. That voice was my Pappi's! It was right! Everything will be alright.

The paramedics had tracked us. I was still loudly praying as they checked my vitals. They told me I had just had an anxiety attack, but I was okay. Being escorted back to the shelter was a relief. They were so happy to see us. Although we had missed curfew and dinner, they feed us, embraced us, and told us everything was gonna be alright. In my heart, I knew that they were right.

CHAPTER 9
Other Men

Two weeks later, I had finally got a job teaching. I made $7.25 an hour. I took a cab there faithfully every day from 6 am to 6 pm. I was even able to bring my Pappi with me, which eased my anxiety. I am a teacher at heart, and I love children. So, this was a breeze for me. The kids loved me; each day they came running in screaming, "Ms. Dezy!" they felt my love and I was happy to give it. After two days of teaching, the director raised my pay up by 50 cents. I was grateful she allowed the Lord to speak to her and that she listened. To show my appreciation, I got her a card with a picture of us in it. Her smile said a million things. It meant so much that things were headed in the right direction after so long. Counseling would have been okay if I would have just opened up. I didn't want to seem powerless, like a victim of some sort. I was okay. I didn't need anyone telling me what I needed to do. I felt as if I maintained very well. I write, pray, and when times get unbearable, I'll have a Vodka and Cranberry on ice to ease my mind. This has always been my go-to. It has been working thus far, or has it? I didn't entertain the thought much. I just kept at it! I was working saving money, and everything was falling into place!

Six months went by and I was granted acceptance into a transitional living program. Boy, was I excited to be moving into my own place. When we got there, all I saw was long beautiful hardwood floors. They reminded me of the beautiful house we had just left. Pappi was so happy. They gifted us with a box of toys, and he was in his own little world. For the 1st 30 days, I didn't have to pay a bill. All I had to do was continue to save up money. There were so many rules. I was so used to following my own rules I just knew this was going to be hard. But I started off alright. The catch was, I was on my own. They provided no rides, no childcare, no nothing. Instead, they encouraged everyone to reach out to our neighbors in the complex for assistance. Me? Ask someone for help? I had no idea how to do that. I was so used to making it work on my own that I felt lost at the thought of such. But I did it and I tried it; what an utter failure. What I didn't know that I was no longer in Fort Worth but in a different town. When I asked for a ride to work, the ladies explained to me how far that was. They told me it was too much to deal with the traffic. Just a bunch of foolishness I always try to avoid by never asking for help. So, I made it do what it do and was back taking a taxi. Except 62 bucks a day was not something I could afford. Soon after I lost that wonderful job and was back in square one. One of the requirements was that I had to work, and another Pappi had to attend school. I ran through that money so quickly. Even after managing my bills, food, and Pappi needs, I was out in the middle of nowhere with no help. I had to make a move to keep us here, so I put my mind to work.

We were walking back to the apartment from the park and then I met Ricky. He was at a red light and held up traffic, trying to make me laugh. Telling me, I was too pretty to look so mean. We kept walking and he followed us right on over to the next light, which had a parking lot. He turned in and began saying all the things I needed to hear. A 24-year-old girl and her 4-year-old son were getting in the car with a total stranger because she felt okay. That was the 1st step I took back in the wrong direction! That same day he took us to this wonderful restaurant. We ordered whatever we wanted. Right after, he took us shopping, and he got us new coats, new shoes, new everything. I felt like I was with a millionaire, you hear me. So, after that he dropped us off a few blocks away from our apartment. We carried all of our bags in with a pocket full of money into the apartment. I just remember Pappi saying, "OOOEEE my coat is warm!" Man, I was like, I gotta keep this dude around. True enough, the rule was no dating while being in this program. What else was I gonna do? I had no job, no car, and not a dime to my name. I told myself I was only going to fool with him for a little bit because I knew I wasn't yet healed. I just needed him to help me get from point A to B!

I was able to get a job at a nearby restaurant as a waitress. Not my pick for line of work, but it was a job. A few weeks went by and he still was there, helping me every step of the way. Rescuing me is what he used to call it. It felt good to him that I needed him. He felt like my knight and shining armor when truly all he was for me was a stepping stone to my dependency. He took me to his cousin's house and introduced me; before I knew it, we were in his bed having a mighty good time. Later that evening, we were on the phone all night. He wanted to teach me so much, by him being 32. The problem was I had been there and done all of that. He figured since I was 24, he could tell me anything. He had no idea the life I lived. When I wouldn't listen to his way of doing things, he'd throw a huge fit with me. He would ignore me for a good week. Knowing I needed him to get Pappi to and from school. Knowing I would need him to get me to and from work. So, I would be on my own to find a way to work and a way to take Pappi to school. That eventually got me kicked out of the program. I had to pack up our things and find somewhere else to go. It was a week before Christmas and we were back on the streets. But here comes that step in the wrong direction I had made. Ricky flew in to swoop me up, coming to my rescue! He took me down to Louisiana to live with his family. The only folks who I believed that like me were his sister and his sweet grandmother. His sister was truly an angel. She bought Pappi whatever he wanted for Christmas, and even put money in my pocket. She had no idea who I was, but God sent her my way to love me just because. She had no alternative motive; I needed all that from her. We were there for about three weeks until his sister told me to get away from that fool! I wished I could right then and there.

Two days before the New Year came in. He got tired of me, and I was even tired of him. He was pushing me away. He didn't understand what I had been through and my change in heart when I was now back on the street. I was just praying for a way out. All I could do was write.

"OTHER MEN"

I Humble Myself to see the Real you,
And Baby Boo,
Ya making me want to be Thru!

Pushing, and Nagging while playing to Win
Keep it coming,
Cause Baby there is OTHER MEN!

One who yells
I'm his to the Mountains High,
He can't bear to see
a Tear Fall from my Eyes

There he goes Opening My Car Door,
Catching me right before
I hit the floor

Affection to the T,
Only if I'd let him Be,
For me and only

You see

Love isn't Enough for you

Cause time after time you Sit

Whining like a Bitch

BOO HOO!

I am who I am from A-Z!

Don't like it?

Hell should have Bounced Before C

Cuz at the End of the Day,

As long as you do it your Way

Your gonna keep Pushing, Nagging

And Playing to Win

Cool,

Just know you Honestly Pushing Me

INTO THE ARMS OF OTHER MEN!

I had a job lined up back in Texas, and the plan was for us to go to Texas to a hotel. Work and save up enough money to get our own. Instead, Ricky drove us to Texas, paid up the room for two weeks, and left, never looking back. Pappi and I were in this room, eating some cold fries before we drifted off to sleep as I heard the countdown to 2015 play faintly on the TV! It was now 2015. Pappi and I were bringing in the New Year, scared, not knowing what would come next.

We had one more day left in our stay before our time was up. Deja vu all over again. My Mommy (Taylor) came through; she paid us up for another week. I tried to call back home to get money from my family, but no one had it. I quickly remembered how it was when I was the one who they came to for financial support. They didn't have it then to give back to me, what makes me think they had it now to send for us. I even asked my daddy, but he was still on some I told you so kind of mess.

I got up and we walked around looking for a grocery store to spend my last 20 bucks wisely. We had no luck, yet a thousand raindrops fell on our head, drenching us in an instant. An older lady pulled over to ask us if we needed a ride. I grabbed Pappi and jumped in immediately. She took us back to our room, gave me an umbrella, and wished us good luck.

By the end of the week, I got us into another shelter. This time I was determined to make God proud. I got Pappi into school and walked him there each day. I stayed at the job center; here we were on a strict timeline. In 30 days, you had to be out. So, I busted my tail. Thank God it was tax time. I filled my return and received just enough to buy us a car with cash. A 2002 Grand Am got us around!

I met some awesome ladies in the shelter. All with amazing stories and kept me inspired. We all were in the same boat; we all helped each other out and loved each other just because we could! My time had ended there. I didn't have enough money yet to move into an apartment. Instead of us going on the street, we were able to go live with one of the beautiful ladies we met there. I worked at Amazon as a picker while Pappi was in school. I had just enough time to pick him up and head on over to the daycare job, where I was able to take Pappi with me. We were there until midnight every day. While the kids slept, I read this awesome self-help book called "A Princess in Waiting." It taught me who I was, What I was Worth, and how to show the world I knew it. After I finished that book, I begin to apply it in all I did. The way I walked, held my head up, even the way I responded to guys trying to talk to me. They were saying and doing all the right things, but I knew now that wasn't enough. I started to be told, I thought I was better than them, I am trying to play them and every other thing you could possibly think. Honey, Pappi and I had peace and was not about to let it be disturbed for anything! A man would pay bills for me, splash so much money our way, all in the hopes of getting in where they fit it. But, I learned, it took so much more than that. They didn't realize it, so me, myself and I kept it moving. The right one would come along soon enough!

CHAPTER 10
My First Apartment

After I saved up enough money, we moved into our first studio apartment! I called it our own little box; $675 a month, all bills paid. It ended up being in a different town, but I did not mind driving 30 minutes to take my Pappi to school. That way, he didn't have to keep experiencing so much change. All we had was some blankets, pillows to lay on, and our famous Laptop that help me keep my Pappi at peace. We slipped in a DVD that we had rented from the Library and cuddled up like a baby! That was one night we slept like there was no tomorrow. I remember when our eyes, opened the sun was gone. For a second, I thought, *"Dang. That was a lil' ol' cat nap."* After looking at my cell phone, I noticed it was the next evening. We had slept well over 12 hours. I fixed him some chicken nuggets and me some noodles; then we were back cuddling, falling right back off to sleep.

Months went by as we were blessed with furniture from the Good Will. It was time to decorate then I realized I had left my pictures back in Sunnyvale. So, I took off a week from both jobs and headed to Sunnyvale to visit. The drive back was such a breeze, especially that I knew I was already established in Texas.

Pappi's birthday was in four days on April 1st! So, I got to planning to make this a memorable birthday. We had him a birthday party at the bowling alley and he had a room full of cousins who came to celebrate with him. Oh, he was so happy! It was all I ever wanted for him. We went to spend the night with Tee Tee and Granny our first night. Me and Granny stayed up all night talking like two little schoolgirls. We reminisced about Brian, Hammer, everything. I ended up falling asleep still talking in my sleep; it was hilarious.

The next few days I spent at my cousin Teddy's house. Pappi was with Shantel and his favorite cousin Kingston. There we had so much fun. I ended up getting on the dating app, for Texas, of course, and the dings came rolling in. I had options, baby; do you hear me? I was in control as men sweated me day in and day out just to get to know me. My profile was off the chain. I said what I meant and meant what I said.

"A Princess in waiting for her Boaz" I am worth more than diamonds said the Creator of all things. So, if you can't treat me as such, don't bother hitting me up."

I let them simmer on Read looking at my profile until I got back to Texas. Except for this one guy Louis. Something tugged at me to get to know him. I started a conversation with him immediately. Not sure why, but something stuck out about him. I let my cousin hear all he had to say and we both were like, "AWE OKAY." We talked all night, and he played this wedding song for me by 3 Piece.

As he played that song, he says, "You gonna hear that song again."

I am like, "Boy please, you don't even know me."

He said, "But I do."

I left it at that because, as always, "You can make your mouth say anything." So, after that conversation I let him continue to compete with the other guys on Read!

Then here come Johnny calling me; I guess he thought I was some sort of the same ol' vulnerable girl that left Sunnyvale over a year ago. I wasn't! But I was gonna play along. So, I go on over there to where he was, of course, he only wanted some sex from me. In return, I only wanted some "oral" from him. So, there we are he was surprised that I didn't give in and give him nun and me laughing inside for the attempt I made of him satisfying me in bed. I must have been out of my mind to expect something like that. He told me, "Man, you trying to play me like I'm just a random dude out here." In my head, I wanted to say, well, you are. But instead, I frowned in disgust as we tried to have a natural conversation. It felt too awkward, so I just saw myself to the door.

Seeing my other cousin, Monique, was such a joy. It used to be the three of us; me, her, and Teddy. We stayed hanging. We knew each other's weaknesses.

As she saw me coming out of there, she said, "Ms. Rita, I hope you didn't give homie none."

I laughed at the thought of that and said, "Hell Nawl, just seeing if he had changed."

As we hugged and parted, ways she told me how much she loved me and was so proud of me. It meant so much. Although we grew apart and we lost contact, great memories like that will forever reign in my spirit!

Making it back over to my Tee Tee's house, Pappi met me as we went to take our yearly pictures. No matter what the year brings, I make it mandatory to capture a family moment. The pictures we had taken went amazing; we smiled as if we were rulers of the world. You couldn't tell what we had just gone through. That was nobody but God giving us smiles of triumph.

We said our Goodbyes, this time, it was easier because I told them I'd be back to visit next year. They trusted my word. As we packed our things to go, there was my daddy coming to see us off. He didn't say much, just stared at us for what seemed like forever. Then he reached out to hug us both in love and walked on back to his car. Driving off, all we heard was a "beep-beep" coming from his car. We got a glimpse of his unknown emotions pouring down his face. As he quickly turned his head, going back from where he came.

CHAPTER 11
My Dream Man

Making it back to our cozy apartment, we both sighed in relief. Pappi says, well, that was fun as he put on his PJs and jumped on his bed. I went to stand in my bathroom mirror just starring at myself. I had to get a good look at the girl who had made it thus far in one piece.

I heard a voice yell, "Time for a drink!' As I toasted to myself in my new studio apartment mirror.

I winked at myself and said, *"That voice was you, girl!"* and I was right!

I kept grinding, working focused on us, I kept being chased by these guys. But that one guy Louis was definitely winning the race. He wanted nothing from me. We talked, talked, and then talked some more until one day he wanted to come to see me. Pappi was fast so sleep and here was this Big Hunk of Chocolate bringing me a hot meal. We ate, laughed, talked about everything. Of course, he wanted some of my good stuff but, he respected my wishes.

5 a.m. came around and I told him he had to go before my Pappi woke up and he did as I asked. From that point on, he treated me just as I demanded to be treated, like a Queen. We dated for a few months before he experienced some hardships and wanted to come live with us. I told him in order to come live up in here you have to pay all these bills two months in advance because that's how I got it set up. He did just that and we started evolving.

"MR. DREAM MAN"

Last night I Dreamed, Dreamed

Yes, Dreamed of You

Woke up Wishing,

Will this come true?

Standing there Holding my Hand

Could he be my DREAM MAN?

Kissing me ALWAYS feels right,

Walking away when he is Angry,

He doesn't want to Fight

Yes! He knows how to Make Love to me

Wrapping me in his Arms

For what feels like Eternity

Oh, Love NEVER Felt So Good

Clicking my Heals together,

Chanting silently

I WISH, I WISH, I WISH YOU WOULD

Tell me it's all going to be Okay,

Promise me you will Help

Take the Pain Away

YES MR. DREAM MAN

Clutching on so Tightly, to my Hand

Family time is the Key,

Your never Concerned about just yourself,

It's always a We!

MR. DREAM MAN,

Seems as if he is Right in the Palm of my Hand

But then you begin to Fade Away

I'M SCREAMING NO, NO, NO!

COME BACK DAMN IT!

YOU'RE GOING THE WRONG WAY!

Drifting, Floating away you went

Damn, why in the Hell did you have to Quit?

I wake up looking Puzzled

Just my Luck,

Thinking I caught a Win

But here I am still Waiting On

MR. DREAM MAN

CHAPTER 12
Louis

Things were good, he took me about an hour and a half to meet his first-born son and my heart began to ache. He was a year younger than Pappi, but you would not think he was after talking to him. Something was wrong in that house. That baby boy deserved better. I had told myself then, *"That I was going to get custody of him."* But before any of that could happen. Here comes CPS (Child Protective Services) calling us, telling us to come down to the courthouse because all the kids had been taken out of his mother's custody. We took off work and flew to his rescue. As we passed them in the lobby, we heard a little voice whisper, "Daddy." Louis went over to pick him up and all you saw were gums smiling from ear to ear. He was happy to be embraced by us. I gave him a tight hug and from that day on, he was now ours.

I had Pappi in school but still working at a Child Care Center, so I was able to take him with me. OMG, that is when so many things were revealed. He was in a separate class than I taught, so the teacher had already assessed him. He had a very severe speech disorder. All signs pointed to Autism and a severe intellectual disability. I grew so angry with Louis.

I explained to him, "This is your son; how could you sit and allow him to go through this and not get help? I don't care how much she didn't want you to see him. You are his Father." All he could do was say your right, looking so pitiful in the face.

We drove him back to the apartment where his sister had been staying with us with her infant baby girl. From one lady to another, I knew she didn't know her worth. I had already been there done that, but I kept my judgment and comments to myself. Her whole point in coming to Texas from a little small town in Arkansas was to better herself. Not worry about the relationship her brother had going on. I mean, the town they are from is a little old country town. When you read about dirt roads and red dirt with farms all around, picture this country old town.

One day Louis said, "I want to take you and Pappi somewhere."

I was like, "Cool."

So, we all got in his car and six hours later, we were pulling up to a trailer home that looked to be in the middle of nowhere. It was his Mother's house. She was so polite. I'm telling you, I felt like I was getting the royal treatment from her. She cooked for us, made sure we were comfortable and even took me around the small town. The tour was literally over in 5 minutes.

The next morning, we woke up and went to their church. Very refreshing to see she was a woman of God. We didn't talk much in detail about anything in particular, but she gave off great vibes.

Back at our apartment, Pappi and I had made it our sanctuary. I hadn't let Louis call it his own yet. I only allowed his sister to come because Louis explained the relationship she was in and how she needed to get away. He had to earn that title, just like we did. I figured it wouldn't be soon. Only because every other day I would be fussing at him for silly little mistakes. Like telling a random girl on Facebook how good she looks. I was constantly letting him know I wasn't taking even the smallest unintentional disrespect. He was confused.

He would always say, "I don't mean it to be disrespectful; it's just what I am used to." He was allowed to do it in his other relationships. Hell, I may even would have went for anything before now. But now. I KNEW WHO I WAS! He was in for a full ride with me. Anytime he even looked like he wasn't cool with my request of how I want to be treated, I quickly showed him the door. But he didn't go. In fact, he did all he could to meet my request to be treated like a Queen, even when it came down to his sister. You see, his sister and him seemed to be day and night. Every other word was a curse word; she was always angry, super ungrateful, and gave off a bad vibe. I don't know what she had been through. But she had to take the first step if she wanted better, just like I learned I had to do. She had something about my Pappi and from that moment on, I was ready for her to go. Disrupting the little bit of peace we just got was the last thing she was gonna do. On top of that, she was still fooling with the no-good guy, who I thought I was helping get her away. Oh, no. I can't help anyone who isn't willing to help themselves, and I was done. I gave her a 30-day notice and she agreed. Louis and I talked about it every night and he agreed as well. I don't know if it was just to make me happy or if he really believed she needed a push. It sure wasn't because of my good loving. Hell, he knew he had to marry me to get in where he fit in, in that department. He knew I said what I meant and meant what I said.

One day his sister wanted to use his phone and happen to see texts of our conversation and went off the deep in. I didn't care. That was our sanctuary, and NO ONE was going to violate it! I went to work the next day on one. Then here comes the lady I was working with picking with me as if I was some sort of punching bag. Baby, before you knew it, I had blown up on everybody. I remember his sister coming to me like, so what you want to do, you want to fight or what? I was lying in my bed. I am not sure what her or the girl at work thought.

But I said boldly, "it's whatever to me."

I will protect our peace at all cost. We have been through too much to get here for some non-factor to come to mess with it. I had posted this status on social media.

Venting on my page, saying, *"Folks swear because I am quiet, I am scary. But back me up in a corner and see how I come out swinging."* Oh, and here comes his family.

They were all replying, "Say it to her face, don't be scared!"

Baby, I fought a man twice my size without hesitation. Scared of what? Oh, did they swear I was directing that right to his sister? Me, myself didn't give a damn.

I fell back from all of them and told Louis, "Look, Bro, I didn't go through Hell and back to get a tiny bit of piece just for you and your folks to come to take it away from me. I gave him no option." I told him if they were not Pappi and I, they had to go. Then I rolled on off to sleep with no worries, no regrets, and feeling A-Okay.

Halfway through the night, I heard him giving her a speech about how he loves me, how I am always there for him, and so on and so on. I laughed because I heard the disbelief in his sister's voice. I didn't stay up for the entertainment; I drifted right back off to sleep. All I know is she was gone shortly after. She kept saying how she was the one who raised him as if he owed her something, but at the end of the day, we are all grown and must take accountability for our own actions. What it was is, she felt as if Pappi were mistreating Jay. I assured them all that I would never let anything happen to him. I am the blessing that allowed Louis to keep him. I am raising these boys. I took pride in that, honey. We all reap what we sow in some sort of form or fashion. I had to learn this lesson the hard way, but you better believe I learned it.

Soon after, I fell in love with Louis. Every now and then, I'd have a flashback of what I put my son and I through and he would literally wrap me in his arms and rock me to sleep humming gospel songs. Before I could think of it, he did it for my heart. He was literally the opposite of Johnny. We both loved the Lord; we'd sit up reading the Bible then discussing what we thought about it. We both enjoyed some good old blues and a nice cocktail. True enough, I had to stay on him about silly mistakes; you would think he'd know better than doing. But overall, he was my "Superman." His father and stepmom lived near, we would go over there sometimes, and I remember being asked if I had an anger problem probably because I was always going off on him.

"No, no anger problem here. I just have finally been able to realize I am the bomb.com. So, anything under the bomb.com would not be tolerated."

It was so funny that I was done correcting him. I wanted out but something kept telling me to stay. This man wanted to marry me; I was not sure at all. I prayed, fasted and there was that voice again telling me, "I got you."

Fourteen days later, our two boys joined us at a park on New Year's Eve in front of a beautiful lake as we said, "I Do!"

CHAPTER 13
A New Place

Finally, moving out of that studio apartment, we found a 2-bedroom duplex. A new year, new place, new family. I struggled with Jay so much as I took him with me to school. He had severe issues I had never dealt with and didn't know how to. All he did was scream in the next room. Finally, I was able to get him into Head Start, where they came through and showed out. I received so many resources it was unbelievable how much of a change we saw; Speech Therapy, Play Therapy, and all. He began to settle in more and has been thriving ever since.

Then I started working for the same company as a Teen Mom Advocate. I fell in love with those girls. They loved me because I could relate to what they were going through. I was an ear when they needed it, a ride to work to avoid stress. My past mistakes saved them from making some future ones. I was just there and loved every minute of it. Being able to love just because. God had put me in a place where I had something more to live for than just being a mother. I walked in my purpose daily!

Then there was Copresia, a 15-year-old young lady with two kids. Who inspired me to the fullest? She was one of the girls on my caseload. Her mother had put her out for whatever reason, and she was homeless. Not able to cross that line of professionalism the Lord birthed a Non-Profit Organization out of me called L.O.V.E. (Leaning On Virtuous Energy). This name came about as I wondered how we made it through all we did. The only thing that made sense was leaning on virtuous (meaning good, meaning Godly, meaning kind) energy! I wanted to teach these teens how to do that in the midst of hell. I wanted to give them a place to call home when they weren't sure where else to go. I wanted to demonstrate virtuous love by meeting the physical, mental, and spiritual needs of at-risk youth! That is my mission. I helped this young lady through my organization get back on her feet. I provided resources as well as 1st and last months' rent for her first apartment. She needed me, and I needed her to know that God was in control. She found herself a church that fits her and grew in the Lord. I thanked God for speaking to me, and then I took pride in being obedient to do all He commanded me.

A few months later, I was planning a wedding back home for us. Yes, we were already married, but it was important to have my family celebrate with us despite the past. Johnny had decided to come around to be "Daddy" to Pappi. Calling him on the phone and sending gifts to him totally surprised me. It made Pappi happy to be able to say his Dad was in Sunnyvale when one of his friends asked, versus not knowing. I wasn't going to take that away from him. He knew that he wasn't his real dad. But taking pride in calling him such so I just let him be.

I was still in contact via phone with my birth mom, she contacted me and told me I had an Auntie who lived in Houston.

I was thinking, *Oh Lord, I am good on that note."*

But when I talked to her, I knew she was different. The way she talked said intelligent, the way she laughed said delightful and I just wanted to be in the midst of that. She didn't know me from Adam nor Eve but was all in to help me with this wedding. She loved me just because and I vowed to never let her loose.

Taking my husband and the two boys to Sunnyvale was a quick task.

Louis got us there way quicker than I could have ever. There we were pulling up to my Tee Tee house. They were happy to see all of us as they embraced us. My Tee Tee was my Matron of Honor. She was ready for me; she had all the fixings decorated. All the bride hats and glasses I could ask for. We partied. The next day, Shantel took us out to the club and put us in VIP; we partied a bit more.

Then on to the actual wedding rehearsal. My auntie from Texas walked in like a million bucks. Turning heads, do you hear me? It tickled me to hear them calling her boogie and what not. Please, she was the stuff, knew it, and wasn't afraid to flaunt it. Behind her came my Birth Mama. She looked how I dreamed she would look the day I was reunited with her. She had on some bad heels, a beautiful dress, hair done, and a face full of makeup. I knew that was my aunties doing. But I let her have the credit. My Daddy was being a spoiled brat as usual, and I was over it. He made sure the world knew he was not going to walk me down the aisle because I didn't allow Louis to call and ask for his permission to marry me. Louis wanted to, but I stopped him. What has he done to earn that right to decide who I marry and don't? He went to God for permission, and it was granted the moment I said I Do! I had decided my boys would walk me down the aisle and left it at that.

The wedding day came, and my Mommy and the crew came to support me. My Mommy (Taylor) and the girls cooked all the food. They were not in my wedding as I hoped they would be, but they were there. To me, it was a disaster, that day, I was so grateful for liquor because I think my Auntie bout gave me the entire bottle to hush me up.

As I walked down the aisle tipsy, I saw his mom giving me such a look of aww; that felt so good. We hadn't said much to each other since the incident with her daughter, but I had a feeling that was going to change. I have always been a lady of principal. Right is right and wrong is wrong. But some folks feel like they will ride for their kids, right or wrong! Not me! If my boys mess up, I am going to tell them and encourage them to get it right. But as always, to each its own!

The next person who caught my eye was my husband. He stood there looking so mad that if I hadn't been tipsy, it would have made me stop right there in my tracks and say, "Redo!" I deserved a smiling face from my husband as I walked down the aisle. But I was in my own little world singing my India Arie to myself. *"Because he is the truth said he is so real, and I love the way that he makes me feel"* As I climbed the stairs, I started instantly being goofy with him. On the low, it worked, and I got him to smile. I read my poem to him and we said our fake I dos! I later found out that he was upset because the folks had messed up his walk down song. I know how he can dwell on something when he is upset, so I requested the waiter to get him another drink!

On to the reception was even a bigger disaster. Someone from my own family went into my Bridal suite and cleaned out all the lady's purses. I was determined not to let that ruin my day, so I acted as if it didn't happen. Then there went my cousin Nika out on the Dance floor and started yelling. She may be deaf, but she went off about her money being stolen out of her purse. After my husband saw that he went right out there on the dance floor behind her telling everyone they better cough up the money or it will be a search as you walk out these doors. He made them feel some type of way I tell you. I saw it in their faces, family or not, it was to be expected. After such an upsetting event, I asked the DJ to wrap it up early. I was ready to go back to good ol' Texas! Where I wouldn't allow myself to be surrounded by folks who would ruin such a special day for their own selfish reasons.

One of my Aunties asked if I would join them and go out to the club to celebrate, after that, all I wanted to do was go to sleep. We made it back to the room and fell off to sleep in our wedding attire.

We were awakened to his Mom dropping off the boys on her way to the highway. We said our goodbyes and did the same thing. Ready to knock out these 1,717 miles back to our home in Fort Worth, Texas!

CHAPTER 14

How You Came About

Louis wanted me to have his child so badly, but I was not ready. He wasn't ready either. He hadn't proved himself worthy enough to have a child with me. He was struggling being a full-time dad to the boys. It was always me! So that was the last thing on my mind. He would beg and pled, so I asked him why he wanted one by me so badly at the time.

His reply was, "So that we would always be connected."

I didn't understand that answer until a week later. The Baby Mama had posted something on social media pertaining to my husband and her sleeping together. I politely contacted her for details, not an angry nor disrespectful bone in my body. She sent me all the proof I needed. It turns out before we were married, they had been fooling around with each other. I grew so angry at God. Questioning The Great I Am! *Wondering why in the world did You command me to marry this man? Why didn't You allow me to leave when I wanted out?*

My heart was broken so badly! The love I once had for him was gone. No matter how many tears he shed, not many how many times he begged and tried to make it right. He had lost my entire heart and he knew it. The Lord waited until I made a covenant to this man before Him "for better or worse," then allowed me to find out. I believe He did that because He knew how I loved. He knew what kind of woman I was. It wasn't about Louis and me; it was about the Lord and me. He put me where He needed me for His own reasons. He knows the beginning at the end and the end at the beginning. My God told me to stay put; He had something big in store for me. So, I did just that. What I should've done was found some sort of counseling for myself. But I didn't. My health problems came back because I swept this pain under the rug, acting as if it didn't happen. Until two days later, my cycle was late. I was in the ER for my blood pressure being so high and here come these folks telling me I was pregnant. I cried silently.

"This damn fool done got me," I said to myself.

He wanted a guaranteed connection to me, as he said. I realized why now. Because he was up to no good beforehand and knew I had found out. Having his child would mean he would always be connected to me in some sort of way.

I felt played as I told the doctor while in tears, "This was the last thing on earth I needed!"

I was still working as a Teen Mom Advocate in the office, looking like one. My pain turned into hidden depression. I drifted away from Louis and my marriage began to go down the drain. God had already told me, being where I was, was not about Louis. So, I let it drift away. But as I let that drift away, so did myself. I wasn't taking care of myself as I should. I stopped going to the doctor and my health issues only worsened. I just didn't care anymore. I really did not want this baby, that wore me down alone. Health problems are still hidden; I ended up going into labor two months early. May 12th, here come Ahkhim sliding into this world. It was so quick I didn't even need any medicine. The name Ahkhim came to mind. I looked it up and seen how it means Created by God. I knew I had no doing in that so, the name was perfect.

I was not even able to leave the hospital for another week due to my blood pressure. I was still upset at the fact that I had just had another little boy. But I had to get over it. I took my blessing with a grain of salt. One thing about it for sure, I was tired of being in the hospital. It only gave me more time to think, think, and think some more. Before I knew it, I was signing myself out against the doctor's orders. Only to go to a checkup two days later to be admitted in again. I was over it. I begin to cry all my worries away. Cry all the hurt away that I had constantly been sweeping under the rug. I took it all off me and gave it to God! I couldn't do nothing else with it. I was advised to meditate. So, I grew deep into my India Arie and essential oils to create a safe place. That moment I felt refreshed as they gave me another blood pressure prescription and sent me home with my little boy!

The idea of me giving him a child was still not setting well with me; I just didn't feel like he deserved it. God was still right there, telling me to be still. Reminding me, "I've always had you," Time went by, and all I could was write."

"HOW YOU CAME ABOUT"

Thinking of HOW YOU CAME ABOUT,
All Explanations and Reasons,
I began to Doubt

The Lord promised He'd Deliver
ALL DESIRES OF MY HEART
Then shoooo, you'd think how He ought to know
I WANTED NO PART

With you being Young, Wild, and Free
And me Obeying God to let you Be

A Detour Birthed,
That NEITHER ONE of us was ready for
Not knowing what to do, I heard a still voice saying
BE STILL GIRL, I ALWAYS GOT YOU!

A child shouldn't be born out of
Confusion, Disloyalty, or a Heartache
But Understanding, Commitment and Love

You see, you DON'T DESERVE that part of me
Not to hold his Precious Body at Night
To look at his Beautiful Face,
See me to make your World Alright

Fighting this Battle of Disbelief,
Unfairness, Unwanted,
So unnecessarily

Someone reminded me,
We are one!
This Battle I have Chosen to Fight,
My God has ALREADY Won!

Only a Fool such as Myself,
Would think, this is about You
To even Consider it being about Me

Such a Precious Gift created with Purpose
Still, I ask why
Then I simply "be Still"
As God told me how He feels

Ahkhim: Meaning Created by God
Now Kiss your Tears Goodbye
And STOP asking why

Never forget I sit High and Look Low
Therefore, everything I say
WILL ALWAYS GO!

CHAPTER 15
Live Life to the Fullest

We found this beautiful house and moved right in even though the paperwork was in my name. Therefore, the lady would not let me have the house until she was confident, I had a husband who would live there with me. It all started to make sense. After we got all our things in, I sat in our huge back yard staring up at the stars. I whispered, "Okay, I see you God," anything I wanted physically, mentally, spiritually, I had it! I was more financially stable than I had ever been, and I couldn't figure out how. I knew it was those awesome budgeting skills I had acquired as an independent teenager. I was being blessed out of nowhere. Like no lie, checks wrote out to me from places I have never been that would say I overpaid in fees. Or just random folks wanting to bless me. I received free counseling and really started my healing process. My nonprofit was being a blessing to others, and I had now transitioned into a teaching role with the same company. I had an amazing co-teacher; Blakely was her name. She helped me so much spiritually; a lady who knew all my issues but never once judged me. She loved me just because and working with her was like being at home, FULL Of LOVE.

Well, five years later, my school closed. I've always taken pride in being a mother first! It was always just the boys and me. Louis was always working. The boys and I had an unstoppable bond. I raised them my way! I would make that clear to every friend, boss, and family member I ever had. So, if it didn't fit in comfortable enough for me to be the mother I needed to be to my boys, it just wasn't even up for discussion. I stood tall on that one. A lot of folks don't understand the way I parent, and that is alright because I say it time and time again. These are "My Boys" I don't love one more than I love the other. They are all my boys. I work hard day in and out to ensure there is a legacy left behind when I go that can be passed down from generation to generation.

I remember this one time the boys were fighting each other. I mean, like really fighting (in their eyes). I recorded it to show Louis how they were behaving. To me, it was just brothers fighting. I made them stop and then talked to them about what they had done and how they had felt about it. They apologized to each other as brothers should. But then the family saw the clip and just knew I was out to allow Pappi to hurt Jay because they were not blood brothers. Jay is the typical little brother who annoys his big brother. Pappi is the typical big brother who gets annoyed by his little brother. I allow them to be brothers my way. When I sincerely talk to them, there is no place they'd rather be. So, I must be doing something right. Each time I sit up and think about what kind of mother I am to them, I smile. There isn't anything I'd change! I love being their mother! That is why when it came time to move me to another school that was too far from my boys. That was a no! Even though the alternative to that was no money, no job, no paying bills. I had to. My boys came first in everything I did! I was so stressed and worried. But I had learned how to meditate and tap into my greater being that I knew exactly what to do. I went on a fast to get some clarification and there was the Lord saying so boldly, "Open your own school!"

Afraid of using the last savings I had for the bills in case it didn't work out. Louis encouraged me; he knew I had it! So, I stepped out on my faith.

A month went by without any children. I didn't fret, not one bit. Before I knew it, Ms. Dezy House Of Love was in business. I get to teach my way. I have fun with my sugars. When they step through my door, I make sure they feel how happy I am that they are there. When they leave, I make sure they know exactly how much I care. God commanded me to come to Texas to live out my purpose through my nonprofit by helping youth. God commanded me to Be Still when I wanted to leave my husband. He also wanted me to love these boys that He blessed me to have. My God blessed me with this house because He knew who He created me to be. He knows the end at the beginning.

He said, "Seek me first the Kingdom of Heaven, and All things Will line up!"

Here I am six years later with an entire Nonprofit, growing daily without anything or anyone hindering me. I am valued for doing that just BEING ME! I am surrounded by folks who LIVE THEIR LIFE TO THE FULLEST! THEY LOVE JUST BECAUSE IT FEELS GOOD! Each day I get rewarded tremendously to love a bunch of children Just because!

I am genuinely grateful for every hardship. As I sit here toasting to the New Year with my family. I drift off and I think about these testimonies. Suddenly I hear all our voices yell with satisfaction "Rags to Riches baby, Rags to Riches!" That my friend was the voices of Ms. Dezarita Dashai and her family!

Outro:

Even though I've been through Hell and Back, opening tons of question marks filled doors. I'm still here. I am a living witness who encourages you to step out on your faith and open that door full of question marks! You know you are settling. Whether it be in your job, your environment, or your life all together. Get in touch with your Highest Power and change it! You deserve it! My name is Dezarita Dashai I hope you have more than enjoyed this short story, but, felt inspired enough to LIVE YOUR LIFE TO THE FULLEST, STARTING TODAY!

www.ingramcontent.com/pod-product-compliance
Lightning Source LLC
Chambersburg PA
CBHW071504070526
44578CB00001B/439